The Story of Elizat

Conside1

John Hill

Alpha Editions

This edition published in 2024

ISBN : 9789362920485

Design and Setting By
Alpha Editions
www.alphaedis.com
Email - info@alphaedis.com

THE STORY OF ELIZABETH CANNING CONSIDERED.

Before I speak any thing in support of that Truth, on the Evidence of which the Life of a most injur'd Person depends; I think it necessary, that I may not seem, under the Colour of public Information, to be acting an interested Part, and defending my own Conduct, to say, that I am convinced it needs no Defence. Whatsoever the Malice of little Adversaries may wish to propagate on this Head, I shall be at Ease in my own Mind, while conscious of the Honesty of my Intention; and I have Reason to be satisfied, with Regard to the Opinion of the World, while I have the Honour to be told, that he who is certainly the best Judge, and perhaps the best Person in it, says, that I have done as became a prudent Man.

No one will call it a Bad Action, that I have endeavoured to obtain the Truth, in a Case, where Humanity must have engaged any, who had the least Suspicion of Falshood, to wish the Secret known; it would have been a very imprudent one for him, who had no Authority to have taken that Confession which discovered it; and it has appeared to those who are better Judges, that it was most right, when the Preparation was made for that Confession, to apply to the supreme Magistrate of the Court, in which the Cause had been tried, to receive it. This is all I have done in the Matter.

I claim no Praise from it; that belongs to another; but neither can I regard those who shall think, that which I have done merits Censure.

Being disinterested, I may expect Credit; but there is yet a Reason why I shall speak less freely. 'Tis an unfortunate Circumstance, that with the Innocence of this Person, there is connected the Crime of another; if not the intentional, at least the effectual Crime: The Evidence that absolves the one accuses the other; and it is one of those Incidents, under which Humanity is wounded by the Means, while it glories in the End.

It will be found, however romantic, or however absurd, such Conduct may appear to many, that I have acted in this only on the Principle of real Honesty and public Utility; and as I have acted, I would wish to see others also act. But while I shall plead yet farther in the Cause of a Person who is innocent, whom I have not seen, nor do know that I ever shall see; and in whose Favour, I do avow in the Face of Almighty God, no Application whatsoever has been made to me; it will give me Pain to reflect that in every Argument I am wounding another; concerning whom I know nothing of Certainty, more than appears from this Evidence; nor can judge how far what so appears to be her Guilt, may admit of Palliation.

I know how improper, nay, how dishonest, it is in many Cases to prepossess the Public against those whom their Country has not yet found guilty of any Crime: No History can produce a greater Instance of it than is before us in the present Story; and I shall think the Obligation sacred that restrains my Hand upon every other Occasion: But here the Life of a Person, certainly innocent, is concern'd on the one Part; and not so much as the Life, even should the worst be proved, and the Laws put in their fullest Execution, of one, as certainly a Cause of the greatest Distress, and almost of Death to that Innocent, on the other. As this is the Case in the present Enquiry, the Particularity of the Circumstance may dispense with what would be faulty on a different Occasion.

I must the more think the doing of this necessary, and therefore justifiable, as mean Sophistry, and the Parade of Argument, have been employed on the other Side; and the Attempt of vindicating the Accuser, though but a secondary Consideration, has, with some Persons, altho' I hope with none of Consequence, prevailed against that Proof of Innocence on the Part of the Accused, which alone can prevent the Execution of a Sentence procured by a confess'd Perjury.

I had read the Pamphlet in which these are us'd, as a Justification only of the Conduct of a Man, against whom I have no Resentment; and, as such, I could not desire to invalidate any thing that it contained: But though I had no Wish against its Success on that Account, I cannot see it aiming to overthrow that Justice and Compassion, which were growing up in the Minds of all Men, with Respect to the Object whom I had proposed to them as so worthy of those Emotions, without treating it with that Severity, and condemning it to that Ignominy which it deserves; without detecting its Misrepresentations, refuting its imagined Arguments, and pointing out to those, who have not already seen it, where they are to smile upon its Puerility.

If it be possible that I should by this Piece of Justice make that Man more my Enemy, than he is at present; I tell him, no Part of this is written with that immediate Design: But I shall also add, that the Importance of the Cause will compensate all that his pointless Arms can return upon the Occasion; and that, if I shall become conscious, I have been instrumental, tho' in ever so small a Degree, in saving the Life of an innocent Person, the Remembrance will make me enjoy the Outrages of all his little Followers.

But with the same Warmth, under which I shall feel this Pleasure, I must be sensible of the Pain which will attend the Consciousness, that what I say, may be so construed as to hurt the other. I beg to be believed that I have no Intent, for most assuredly I have none, to injure her: Perhaps I look upon what she has done, with less Severity than others. She may be able to prove that she was somewhere confined, though she was not at this Place: I hope she will prove it: But as many other Accounts may be given how a Person, less innocent, might have been employed, I must have leave to name some of these: I must have leave, till such a Fact is proved, to doubt the Truth of all; and to build the Testimony of the Convict's Innocence, in part, upon the Improbability of what at this Time appears her Story.

Whatsoever I shall advance on this Head, is alledg'd only as what might have happen'd, and I desire it may be understood as meaning no otherwise. I have no particular Knowledge of the Truth with Respect to *Canning*; and therefore can be positive only with Regard to those Proofs that appear of the Convict's Innocence. As this is the true Case, I beg that whatsoever I conjecture, may be received only as Conjecture, and may not hurt her in the Eye of the World.

When Truth is to be decided, Sophistry is impertinent; and when the Proofs are at hand, and are such that all may judge by them, they use a Freedom to which they have little Right, who attempt to guide and to direct Mankind in their Determination. Whatsoever lies within our Knowledge more than others have had Opportunities of acquainting themselves withal, it becomes a Duty to impart; but when that is done, by what Claim is it that we dictate? these or these Sirs! must be the Conclusions: We are to state the Case, the World is to determine.

'Tis hard for him who has engag'd, be it no more than his Opinion on one Part, to be disinterested with respect to the other; nay, if he were unbiass'd, such an one is still but a single Person; and he has little Candour, and less Modesty, if he supposes every Individual of the Publick is not as able as himself to judge upon that which he allows to be, or which he affects to call, clear Evidence.

As many things have come to my Knowledge in this strange Affair, with which the Public cannot have been acquainted; it may be indulged me to speak of them, without the Censure of Officiousness; and as I have already delivered something concerning an Enquiry into the Truth, which, as it appeared the Concern, so it has been the Study of some Persons to invalidate, it may be esteem'd a Duty in me to support that which has already so appeared; and to do this the more fully, I shall add to it what farther the Time, the Nature of the Proceedings, and the Respect to those under whose Cognizance the Whole now remains, may warrant me in disclosing.

I have ordered my Name to be put to this Pamphlet, that I may not be supposed the Writer of those many other Pieces, which Ingenuity, or its Parent Hunger, may hereafter obtrude upon the World; or of some Things that have already offer'd themselves to its Notice; the Motives to which, seem rather to lie in personal Resentment, than an Attachment to Justice. As the Original Papers will hereafter appear, what I shall now propose may stand as an Introduction to them: and it will answer also another Purpose; in that it will, I hope, prevent the imbibing of unjust Prejudices, and false Opinions, whether from the Deluded or the Designing, the Interested or the Ignorant.

The truth is of Importance; and it will be laid open: Till that shall be fully effected, the same Principle which influenc'd me, as unconcerned as any Man could be in the whole Matter, and of all Men the least inclined to enter into Disputes and Quarrels, to undertake the Protection, so far as it lay in my scanty Power, of the Innocent, pleads with me, so far as my Opportunities may permit, and so far as may be consistent with that Character which every Man ought to hold sacred, to prevent farther Error.

There will be those who think me wrong from the Beginning; and were I actuated by their Sentiments only, I should agree with them. It was not prudent to engage unnecessarily, in a Cause that must become a Subject of Debate; but there are Motives superior even to Prudence, and these had, in the present Case, a Right to Attention; Honesty, Humanity, and Love of Justice: These, I hope, I shall always, although it be at the Expence of some Scandal, prefer to that cold Principle; inasmuch as I think it a greater Character to be an honest, than to be a wise Man.

Thus much it may have been necessary, though very unpleasing, to say, with Respect to those Motives which induced an unconcerned Person at all to meddle in this intricate Discovery; since those whose own Hearts do not acknowledge any Thought that has not Self for its Centre, may not (uninformed of the Difference) suppose it possible any others should have Place in the Breast of a Stranger. The Persons are all unknown to me, but the Story was interesting; and Humanity must have been unknown to him, who should have been let into so much of it, as had come to my Knowledge, and not have enquired farther. I could have no Interest in the Event farther than as one Creature of the same Species is concerned in the Welfare of another; nor was I of any Part, unless inclined to pity the miserable Convict; because she was poor, and a Stranger, and oppress'd, and innocent. Such, at least, I was, at that Time, inclin'd to believe her, and I am, by all that has pass'd since, the more confirm'd in that Opinion.

It will appear, that I have weighty, nay, that I have unanswerable and incontrovertible Evidence, that I ought to be so; whenever those sacred Proofs, which at this Time are in the Hands of that generous Magistrate who has obtained them, shall appear, and untill that Time come, perhaps it may not be thought singular in me to be persuaded of the Innocence of this

Woman, from the very Attempts which have been made by those who espouse her Prosecutors, to prove they are not guilty.

I have proposed to consider the whole Story; and to preserve a Conduct answerable to that Intention, I shall begin with it somewhat earlier than those have thought it prudent to do, who have hitherto treated of the Matter. To judge truly of People's Actions, we should enquire into the Designs of them; and this is best done by attending to the earliest Notices.

Some few Days after that *first* of *January*, on which this *little Child*, as those who despairing to convince the Judgment, attempt the Passions of Mankind, affect to call her, is said to have been carried away, I find the following Advertisement in the most Universal of the Daily Papers.

"*Whereas* Elizabeth Cannon *went from her Friends between* Hounsditch *and* Bishopsgate, *on* Monday *last, the 1st Instant, between Nine and Ten o'Clock: Whoever can give any Account where she is, shall have Two Guineas Reward; to be paid by Mrs.* Cannon, *a Sawyer, in* Aldermanbury *Postern, which will be a great Satisfaction to her Mother. She is fresh-colour'd, pitted with the Small-Pox, has a high Forehead, light Eye-brows, about five Foot high, eighteen Years of Age, well set, had on a Masquerade Purple Stuff Gown, a black Petticoat, a white Chip Hat, bound round with Green, a white Apron and Handkerchief, blue Stockings, and Leather Shoes.*

"*Note, It is* supposed *she was* forcibly taken away *by some evil-disposed Person, as she was* heard to shriek out in a Hackney-Coach *in* Bishopsgate-street. *If the Coachman remembers any thing of the Affair, by giving an Account as above, he shall be handsomely rewarded for his Trouble.*"[15:A]

[15:A] Daily Advertiser, January 6.

This is a Circumstance, forgot by the disinterested; and pass'd over, not imprudently, by those who espouse the Girl; but I must declare, that with me it has great Weight. Why supposed to be taken forcibly away? Are these Transactions common? or was there any Thing in the present Case to authorise such an Imagination? To what Purpose should she be forced away! She is not handsome; so that the Design could not be upon her Person; and certainly the Dress that is described so largely, could not tempt any one to carry her off to rob her; nor was it necessary, for that might have been done where she was seized; nay, and in the latter Accounts we are told it was done there.

Who heard her shriek! or what is become of the Hackney-Coach Part of the Story, no Syllable has been since uttered of it. Who should know the Voice of a Servant of no Consideration, calling in a strange Part of the Town from a Coach? What must the Ruffians have been doing who suffer'd her to shriek! or who that heard such a Voice, and did, or that did not know the Person, would not have stopped the Carriage! How came he who heard so much not to call Persons to assist him? there are enough in the Streets at Ten o'Clock; or, where's the Coachman, for Coaches do not drive themselves, and certainly he might be found to justify the Story.

If a Coach carried her, where therefore is the Driver of it? or, if she was dragged along, how did the People, who were taking all this Pains, and running all this Hazard, to no Sort of Purpose, get her undiscovered through the Turnpikes? The Public will judge of this early Advertisement as they think proper; to me the Determination that should be grounded on it appears too obvious; and, perhaps, in due time it will be found supported.

From the Day of this Publication, by which the World was informed that such a Girl was carried off by Ruffians, (a fine Preparative for what has follow'd!) we hear no more of her till her Return at the End of Eight-and-twenty Days; when she tells her absurd, incredible, and most ridiculous Story. A Piece of contradictory Incidents, and most improbable Events; a waking Dream; the Reverie of an Idiot: A Relation that could not be allowed a Face of Likelihood; and that would have taken no hold on any, but as it pleaded to their Compassion.

It was not on the Credit of this Story that the unhappy Creature, in whose Case all these Endeavours have been us'd, was condemn'd. Let us not imagine Courts of Justice swallow such Relations. 'Twas on the most full Account, given by one, who declared that she had seen the whole Transaction of which the Court was concerned to judge. One, who being a Stranger to the Accuser, and a Friend of the Persons accused, declared she saw the Robbery. This was an Evidence which must have been allowed by any Jury of judicious and unbiass'd Men. Now that we are convinced of the Innocence of the Persons who were condemned upon the Credit paid to this Evidence, we must acknowledge, that human Wisdom could not, at that Time, have discovered, nay scarce could have suspected it was false; and that while unsuspected, it had been Injustice not to have done exactly as was done upon the Trial.

We are now reviewing that Account in a very different Light: we have now been let into the Secret of its Origin; we have seen her since voluntarily declare, that it was false and forg'd: not in part false, but in the Whole, and that it was the Off-spring only of her Terrors: and tho' actuated from the Influence of the same Apprehensions, she confirmed it at the Trial, she now declares it, freely and voluntarily declares it, to have been all a Perjury.

She has confessed her Motive to the doing this, and that is it was such an one, as might well have Effect upon an ignorant Creature: This I shall consider at large when I come presently to treat of her Informations. She has declared this to have been her only Motive; and those who are most concerned, do acknowledge, that she was very unwilling to give it; and was very difficultly brought to it. What Reason could she have to contradict it? None! To this no one can speak with more Authority than I: and I declare she had none. It was to myself she promis'd the Confession. I had no Advantages to offer to her, nor any Power to terrify: nor was this done privately; so that there are Witnesses who know how free and perfectly 'twas voluntary. I applied to the Lord Mayor, whom, 'till that Time, I never saw, to receive her Confession: She was sent for; she made it; and the Consequences are natural.

The Lord Mayor had at that Time Proofs in his own Hands, as strong as even this Confession, of the perfect Innocence of the miserable Convict; and he has since received innumerable more; all more precise, and punctual; more firm and more convincing. It can be no Reflection on a Court, in which the Determination is made from Evidence, to plead the Cause of that Innocency, which is proved by the after-discover'd Falsity of such Evidence: Shame on the Folly or Malice that pretends it can, even though you, *Fielding*, have pretended it: nor has any thing been yet publish'd, more than what passed publickly; for the Examinations before the Lord-Mayor have not been made in Corners.

This is a Digression, but the Insinuations of bad Men have made it necessary. I shall return to the Relation. The pretty Innocent, such we should take her to be from the Story, tells us she was tempted strongly: she was promis'd *fine Cloaths*, if she would *go their Way*. This is the Account; and in the Name of Reason let us consider it. The Phrase is an odd and unnatural one; and the fine Cloaths were to be given. By whom? By one who hardly had a Covering for herself, and in a Place where every thing spoke Beggary: Unnatural, ridiculous, and absurd!

There can be no Cause assigned, why Men should drag her many Miles, or why Women lock her up to perish, without the least Advantage, or the least Prospect of Advantage. I wish it could be said there appears no End for which all this might be pretended; although there could be none for which it should be done.

Did the prophetic Spirit of her Virtue foresee exactly the Length of her Confinement? How came she else to proportion, for it's plain she did proportion, her Eating to it? There is, indeed, no Reason why she should not have foreseen it, since the Duration was at her own Pleasure. There appears no Cause why she did not make that Escape the first Night, which she effected on the last Day at Four in the Afternoon: and as it has been thought strange that no one opposed the Persons in the Night in carrying her thither; I shall add, that I think it still more strange no one was let into the Story on her Return. Her Weakness might have made her complain; her Terror speak, and even her Countenance must have occasioned Question. People could not be wanting to this Purpose; for she that could set out in the Afternoon to walk from *Enfield-Wash* to *London*, must be met, overtaken, or seen, by many Hundred Persons: her Figure was singular enough to have drawn the Attention of some of these, her Aspect (as you describe it) of them All: The Story has been enough spoken of to bring such People to attest it, had there been any such; but if any have appeared, it has not come to my Knowledge.

Acts of Cruelty have been practis'd by Ruffians: I grant you so much, mighty Reasoner! but there has been a Motive, the worst of them have never done it otherwise: Their own Safety is the Common Cause, and Cowards are to a Proverb cruel. But here Men endanger'd, and not secur'd their Safety, by the doing it; and had no End to answer when it was done. On the same Principle, before we can believe the Women (who has been condemned) would have run the Hazard of her Confinement, when they knew an Escape so practicable, we must expect to find some Motives to their doing it.

The Cant of the Subscription was her *Virtue*, but there must have been a Face to stamp the Price on That: without it the Commodity's not marketable: Naked Virtue is of no Value unto the Sort of People these have been represented. Besides, had there been even this Temptation, the Gipsey, who is charged with the Crime, could not have any Intent to answer in the obtaining of the Sacrifice. She did not keep the House; and it could not be in Friendship to Mrs. *Wells*, for they were Strangers.

The poor Girl left her Mother plump: This, Sir, is your Account, and this the Partridge-Phrase by which you express it. She returned you say emaciated and black; this was on the 29th of *Jan.* and, on the 1st of *February*, she went down to *Enfield* again: as you say, again. Never were Transitions so quick, as have been those of this miraculous Girl; for she was not black at this Time, upon this 1st of *February*. A Day or two had made an amazing Change; for those who were present tell me, she was at that Time red and white like other People.

There was a Time, when even the warmest Advocates for the pretended Injur'd, gave up all Expectation of Credit from the Nature of the Story, and rested it upon the Weight of Evidence. I think, Sir, you was of the Number, and, for the Credit of your Understanding, I hope you were: That Weight is taken off: that Evidence, it is confess'd, was Perjury. The Story now, therefore, stands on the Footing of its own Credibility; and those who are the most violent in its Favour, have, in Effect, if not in Words, given it up as false: I hope they will do this in every Sense. Humanity, tho' mistaken in its Object, was a Plea sufficient in her Favour when they first countenanc'd her; but Humanity now changes Sides, and the Wretch, who pines under the Sentence, claims its Offices.

Let not the once deluded, and since obstinate Men, conceive they will be supported by the Testimony of the Girl's coming Home in this emaciated Condition, of this black Colour, and with this Aspect of a putrid Carcase: Let them enquire, whether this was the Condition in which she was first seen, and they will find it false: Let them ask themselves, and their own Reason, if a Creature, in such a State, could have walked Home; they will find it as absurd as the rest of the wild Story: and there is as much Moral Certainty that it is false; invented by bad Men to serve Purposes; and countenanc'd by weak ones who believ'd it.

It does not appear, (unless her own contemptible Story can be believ'd) that she was confin'd any where, otherwise than by her own Consent: It is not true that she returned in this dreadful Condition; nor can it be true, that she could have supported Life till she arrived at it, and after that have walked ten Miles immediately, or have been carried as far so very soon after it. That she was not confin'd where she says, is clear beyond all Possibility of Doubting, and there will remain not the least Thought of it, even among her best Friends, as soon as the Proofs, now in the Lord Mayor's Hands, shall appear: In the mean Time, I, who have seen them, say it; and have, I hope, some Right to be believ'd.

Where a Girl, like this, could be; and how employed during the time; is not difficult to imagine. Not with a Lover certainly, say you! You would be happy, Sir, if all you beg should be allowed you. Not with a Lover, Sir! Eighteen, let me remind you, is a critical Age; and what would not a Woman do, that had made an Escape, to recover her own Credit, and screen her Lover. I pretend to no Knowledge of this, as having been the Case with Respect to the Girl of whom I speak; but, if we are to reason, let us do it freely; and what appears so likely?

The Description she gave of the Room in which she had been confined, is urged by you to justify; but, Sir, that Circumstance alone ought to condemn her. Let me not be understood to speak of that Description, which she gave after she had seen it: That Subterfuge may serve for the Excuse of those who will be found to want it. But let us now enquire with better Judgment: Let us, Sir, appeal to that Account she gave before the sitting Alderman, by whom she was first examined; and we shall find it countenance the worst that can be thought against her. Observe the Articles.

She described it to be a *dark* Room; in which she lay upon the *Boards*; in which there was nothing except *a Grate* with a Gown in it; and a *few Pictures* over the Chimney; from which she made her Escape by *forcing down some Boards*, and out of which she had before discovered the Face of a Coachman, through certain *Cracks* in the Side.

Let those who have seen the Room speak whether this was a Description of it. They will answer No. No, not in any one Particular. Far from being *dark*, there are *two Windows* in it. These have Casements which were unfastened, out at which she might have *escaped*, had she been confined in it; so that pulling down of Boards to that Purpose could not be necessary: Out at these also, I suppose, the might have *seen this Coachman*, so that she needed not to peep through Cracks. There was no Grate in the Chimney: so that no body could have been guilty of this most housewifely Trick of putting a Gown in one: Nor were there any Pictures over it. Of the latter there was no Probability to be any, because the House had no Profusion of Furniture, and this was a Room of Lumber: And it is palpable there could have been no Grate in the Chimney of a long Time; for the whole Expanse of it was found covered and overspread with Cobwebs, the Work of many Generations of unmolested Spiders. Oh Providence that assists in these Discoveries!

But though there was not what she said she saw in the Chimney, there was about it, Sir, that which she must have seen, had she been there, and which, had she been there twenty-eight Days, she must have seen often enough to have remembered it; there was a Casement, put up over the Chimney to be out of the Way: and this not newly laid there, for it was also fixed to the Wall by Cobwebs of long Standing.

If this were all, Sir, is not this enough to prove she never was in the Place? But this is little to the rest. There was a Quantity of Hay, near half a Load, there: Surely too large a Matter to have been overlooked, and too important to have been forgotten: And there were a multitude of Things besides; some if not all of which she must have remembered; but not any one of all which she mentioned.

Some who went first down, Neighbours and Men of Credit, who went to countenance and to support her, had heard her Account of the Room, and when they saw it, were convinced that her Description did not at all belong to it: they gave her up, and they are to be found to say so. Some who were too officious, eager to have the Story true, because themselves believed it, got there before her also; these, when they had heard the Objections, rode back Part of the Way to meet her, and after some Conversation with her; after, for, if I may have Leave to conjecture from the Circumstance, that is the least that can be supposed, asking her if there was not Hay there; that is, in Effect, after telling her there was, and that she should have said so; rode back, and, with *Huzza's* of Triumph, cried they were all right yet; for she said now there was Hay in the Room. Was this or could it be an Evidence of Weight with the Impartial? The best Way to determine is to ask one's self the Question. What would it have been to you who are now reading of it?

But let me call up fairly the rest of your Arguments: You shall not say I deal partially with you, by omitting any that seem to yourself of Importance; and you shall hear the World say, so much I'll answer for them, that they are one as important and as conclusive as the other.

You have supposed the Girl not *wicked* enough to have devised such a Deceit: That, God and her own Heart alone can tell; and neither you nor I have Right to judge of it. But you add, and this we both may judge of, That you do not suppose her *witty* enough to have invented the Story. I give you Joy, Sir, of your own Wit, for thinking so! I am very far from entertaining an high Opinion of the Girl's Intellects; but such as they are, I think the Story tallies with them: none but a Fool could have devised so bad a one.

You say 'tis worthy of some Writer of Romances. I love to hear Men talk in Character: no one knows better how much Wit is necessary to the writing of such Books; and, to do Justice to your last Performance, no Man has proved more fully, with how small a Share of it, they may be written.

But I shall follow you through some more of these your supposed Improbabilities; and shew you they are all as probable as these. That she should fix upon a Place *so far from home*, is one of them. That may have been the very Reason why she fixed upon it: To me it would have seemed much more strange, if she had fixed on one that was nearer. The farther off, the farther from Detection.

That Mrs. *Wells*'s House should be particularly hit upon seems strange to you. But Mrs. *Wells*'s was a House of evil Fame, and there was no other such about the Neighbourhood: The Improbability must needs be, therefore, that of their fixing upon any other.

We are asked, How should she know this House, as she approached it? No body ever heard that she did know it, as she approached: And for the famous Question, How she could, among a Number of People, fix upon the *Gipsy* whom she had particularly described before, as the Person that had robbed her? The Answer is a very fatal and severe one; it is that she *had not particularly described her before.* It is palpable she never spoke of her even as a *Gipsy*, though no Woman ever possessed the Colour and the Character of that singular People so strongly: Nor had she given any particular Account of her Face; which, had she ever seen it before, must have been remembered; for it is like that of no human Creature. The lower Part of it affected most remarkably by the Evil: The under Lip of an enormous Thickness; and the Nose such as never before stood in a mortal Countenance.

But these are Trifles: You'll give me up all these: I know you will; for you'll do every Thing you must. You'll give all this and laugh at the Advantage. The Strength is yet behind: These are the Outworks; but I shall overthrow your Citadel. This Evidence of *Hall*, you have reserved to the End; and I have reserved it too. Let us now state it fairly. I'll give it all the Strength you can desire; and when I have done so, I will shew you, but that's unnecessary; I'll explain to the World, how all its false Strength was derived to it. Let us here take it in the whole.

The Account of the Transaction, with respect to the Robbery, you argue must be true, because *Canning* and *Hall* relate it both alike. But all Men see how weak an Argument that is. I will not suppose Mr. *Fielding* can be guilty of designing to impose upon the World in this or any Part of the Case which he has published; and therefore I will call it only a weak Argument. Let us consider the Circumstances under which these Accounts were procured, and we shall see they could not be otherwise than perfectly alike, even tho' they both were false.

We, who suppose the Convict innocent, believe the Account of *Canning* to be a concerted Plan, long laboured, and well inculcated. That she should not vary herself in the relating it, will not therefore be wonderful: And I shall allow you Council! for you are not here acting in any other Character; that if the Evidence *Hall* had made a free and voluntary Confession, without Fear, and without Constraint, and this Confession had in all Points confirmed the Account of the other; and if she had before known nothing of her Story; there would have been all the Argument and all the Weight in it that you would have us grant.

But let me ask you, Sir, for none know better than you do, were these the Circumstances of that Confession? I need not ask you: Your Pamphlet contradicts it. She refused to confess any such thing, you tell us so yourself, throughout six Hours of strong Sollicitation, and she consented to do it at last: Why? She says, and you say the same, it was because she was else to be prosecuted as a Felon.

Let us suppose the Story as we think it: An innocent and an ignorant Creature saw Perjury strong against herself: She saw a Prison the immediate Consequence: She supposed the Oaths that prevailed against her Liberty, though innocent, might also prevail against her Life, though innocent; and, to save herself from the Effects of this Perjury, she submitted to support the Charge it made against others: Against those whom she supposed condemned without her Crime, and whom she thought too certain of Destruction to be injured by any thing she added.

That this was the Case, her own Account, that of the World, and even yours, concur to prove; nay, and the very Consequences prove it. If she had sworn the Truth at this Time, is it, or can it be supposed, that, unawed and untempted (for I had no Authority, and the Lord Mayor has Testimony that he used none with her) is it to be supposed that she would have gone back from it to Falshood? and that she would have done this at a Time when it might have been destructive to herself; and when it could only tend to let loose upon her those whom she had injured, and those whom she always affected at least to fear? Certainly she would not. There could be in Nature no Motive to her doing it; and the most irrational do not act without some Impulse.

But let us ask the Question on the other Part! We shall then find it answered easily. Let us suppose we see, for 'tis most certain we do see such a one, a Person who had been awed by her Ignorance, and Fears, into swearing a Falshood; after having first voluntarily declared, in the same Case, that which was the Truth: we see her conscious that, by that Oath, she had procured the Sentence of Death against a Person whom she knew to be innocent; and we shall not wonder at the Consequence. Who is there lives, so abandoned, that he can say he never felt a Pang of Conscience? The Ideot, the Atheist would in vain attempt to persuade Men of it. Suppose what she had thus sworn to be false, as there are now a Multiplicity of Proofs that it all was false, what are we to imagine must be the Consequences? Unquestionably, Terror, Anguish, and Remorse; Wishes to speak, and Eagerness to do it. Where is the Wonder then that she should snatch at the first Opportunity; that she should be persuaded to do it, even by the most Uneloquent! Where the Wonder that she should thus go back into that Truth which she had late denied; and when she had confessed the Perjury, declare and testify, for she did much more than declare it, her Heart at Ease from that which had been a Burden and a Distress intolerable and insupportable.

This she declares to be the Fact; and what can be more natural? There is as much Face of Truth in her Recantation seen in this Light, as there would be Absurdity if it were looked upon in another.

But their Informations, you repeat, are so alike! Sir, I must tell you, they are too like: why do not you also see it? Indeed the Term *like* is improper; they are not like, for they are in Effect the same: And farther, which is an Observation that must sting somewhere, though these their Informations are thus like, their Evidence upon the Tryal was not so. That we may know whether these could be so like without having a common Truth for their Foundation, let us examine into the Circumstances.

Had *Virtue Hall* ever heard the Story of *Canning* before she gave this Information? For if she had, allowing it all to be false, she would assuredly make it like hers, by repeating the same Circumstances. Let us enquire then, whether she had ever heard the Story? Yes, she had heard it many times. It appears by her Account, and by the Concurrence of all other Testimonies, that she had heard it from *Canning*'s own Mouth at *Enfield* on the 1st of *February*; on the same Day also she says she heard it, and undoubtedly she did, at Mr. *Tyshmaker*'s: For, eight Days after this, the Story of this *Canning*, as herself had repeated it now twice in the Hearing of this *Hall*, was published in the News-Papers, to raise Subscriptions. *Hall* can read; or, if she could not, she had Ears, and she must have heard this from all who came to her.

Now let us see when 'twas she gave this weighty Information. 'Twas after all this Opportunity of knowing what it was *Canning* said; 'twas on the fourteenth of *February*, and not before, that she was examined by Mr. *Fielding*. There, as himself informs us, she was under Examination from six to twelve at Night, and then, after many hard Struggles and stout Denials, such are his own Words, she did, what? why she put her Mark to an Information; and swore what it contained was true. What it contained was the same that contained which had before been sworn by *Canning*. The same Person drew both; and that not the Magistrate, no, nor his Clerk: Who then?—why the Attorney who was engaged to manage the Prosecution.

Now, Syllogist, where is your Argument! Can two Persons who swear the same thing agree in all Particulars, and yet that thing be false? Yes certainly, if one has heard the other's Story. As certainly if the same Hand drew up both the Informations, and both that swear are perjured. This is the true State of the Question: You beg too much, as you have put it.

But let us see how these, who agreed so well in the written Informations, agreed in verbal Evidence. We shall find they did not coincide in that; and we shall find a Court of Justice is not satisfied with a few Questions.

Let those who would know this examine the printed Tryal. They will, in that, find *Canning* swearing that no body came into the Room all the time she was there, and that she found the Pitcher there: And they will find *Hall* swearing that the Pitcher was put into the Room three Hours afterward by the Gipsy. They will find tho' both agree in the Fact, yet a Difference in the Circumstances even of the Robbery: *Canning* swears the two Men took her

Stays and went out, while she was yet below; but *Hall* swears this was done after she was put up into the Room.

These things, and things like these, I doubt not influenced that worthy Magistrate first to suspect the Truth, who has now proved the Falsity of both their Evidences. These things were not hidden, Sir, from you: How was it that you overlooked them when you wrote this Pamphlet? All I have urged you know; and knew before. You will find it will convince the World, why did it not take that Effect on you? Are you convinced now that you see it here? Speak freely; and answer to the World this one plain Question, Was it your Head, or what was it that played you false before?

None will wonder, Sir, that Informations thus taken, and under these Circumstances, should agree in all things, even though both were false; nor was it possible for the Jury, on hearing the Evidence of both agreeing in general with these Informations, to do other than find the Accused guilty. None wondered at it, nor will wonder: None were ever weak enough, or wicked enough, to reflect upon them. But although they saw nothing to contradict the Truth of all this Swearing, you did, and you acknowledge it: You acknowledge there came before you something to contradict it, and it deserved its Weight.

Canning's Story appeared improbable; all rested upon the Evidence of *Hall*: And there was given to you, against that Evidence, the Oath of *Judith Natus*, one not belonging to the Gipsies, and whom you have not any Reason to apprehend belonging to them; an honest Woman, Wife of an honest Labourer, who, with her Husband, lay in the very Room, in which the Girl pretended to have been confined, during the whole time of that alledged Confinement. Here was the Evidence of a Person of honest Character, and quite disinterested, against that of *Virtue Hall*, confessed of bad Character, and deeply interested. This Oath, Sir, you will find was Truth: It will be seen: It will be proved that it was so, by Evidence the most incontestible. In the mean time, let me, in the Name of Virtue and Impartiality, ask the whole World whether this free Oath of an unconcerned Person, or the hardly-obtained Information of one who was interested, and had the Alternative only of that Information or a Prison, deserves the most Respect?

You ask, Sir, why this Woman, and with her this Husband, were not produced upon the Tryal? You tell us you can give but one Answer to this, and that you conceal, Sir, I can give another, and it shall stand openly. The Reason is a plain, and 'tis a dreadful one. They were subpœna'd, and they were ready at the Court; but the Mob without-doors had been so exasperated against all that should appear on the Part of the Accused, that they were prevented from getting in, and treated themselves like Criminals.

This is now known, notoriously and generally known; nor is the Cause a Secret. The Public were prejudiced in the most unfair Manner: nor the Public only. Printed Papers were handed about the Court at the time of the Tryal, calculated to enflame every body against the Accused; even those on whose Impartiality the public Justice was to depend. I do not suppose they took such Effect; but that this was the Design is plain. It was an Insolence unprecedented, and surely will never be again attempted.

If Means like these were used within-doors, we cannot doubt enough were employed without; nor wonder that those who could have proved the Innocence of the Accused were insulted, terrified, and driven away. 'Tis easy to know what must be the Fate of the Guiltless, when only those are to appear who accuse them.

Such is the State, and the exact State, of that Case, into which a Suspicion of Misinformation at first, a Confession of Perjury afterwards, and accumulated Proofs in Support of that Confession, have engaged the Lord Mayor of the City of *London* to enquire certainly in a virtuous and laudable Manner, even after the Tryal. The Enquiry has answered all his Lordship's Expectations; the Evidence is clear, and the Proof is full. But for this his impartial Enquiry, made for the sake of Justice only, he is attacked by Calumny and private Prejudice: The envious Hint he must be interested in it; while others, whose Honour is as far beneath his, as their Abilities are inferior, wish the Convict guilty, that he may sink into an Equality. That Magistrate is too well informed of the Respect due to his Sovereign, not to lay all the Evidences first before him; afterwards the whole World will see them: And it is on Certainty and Knowledge I speak, who now tell them, that, when they do see them, they will be convinced at full.

In the mean time, it is not necessary that others should be blamed. Those who are of the contrary Opinion maintain it, because they are ignorant what are the Proofs on which the Innocence of the Convict is supported. Every Magistrate who has enquired into the Story has a Right to Praise from the World for that Enquiry: he has a Right to this, and in Proportion, not to the Success, for that was not in his Hands, but to the Pains which he has taken, and the Impartiality by which he has been governed, in the Endeavour.

Those who set on foot the Contribution, engaged in it beyond a Doubt as an Act of Justice and of Virtue; it is most certain that they have had no other Motive: that they have been imposed on is as certain; but for that others must be answerable. If it were Justice to establish the Subscription, all was Charity and Benevolence in those who encouraged and promoted it; nor is their Generosity, the Motive to which is so palpable and so noble, at all affected by the ill Use to which it might have been applied.

But while these all stand not only excused but applauded, there certainly is one to whom that Tribute is due in a superior Degree; and it shall never be my Crime to mention the Transaction, and omit to pay it. While I see the Lord Mayor in this just and honourable Light, it gives me Pain to find those who are, in all Senses of the Word so vastly his Inferiors, and you, Sir! most of all, placing themselves as it were on an Equality with him: and when I consider, for I know it is so, that his Lordship has, from no other Principle but Humanity and a Love of Justice, undertaken one of the most arduous Tasks that could have been imposed on Man; and this at his own private Expence, and by his own Labour and inconceivable Trouble: when I see him compleating what so good a Heart had designed, by a Discernment equal to his Candour, I own, and, as I am a Stranger and disinterested, I glory in owning it, I see, with all that Indignation which Honesty conceives at the low Cunning of the Base and Wicked, Insinuations, for there are such Insinuations spread, that *foul* and *unjustifiable* Practices have been used since the Tryal. You, Mr. *Fielding*, among others, say this: But I must tell those who invent, and those who can give Credit to it, that the Discernment of this honourable Magistrate is as much above being imposed on by such Artifices, as his Honour would be above encouraging them.

It gives me Pain, when I hear Men talk of *this Side* as their own, and of some other as his *Lordship*'s. He is of no Side or Party; nor has (so I have heard him often say, and so I am convinced) the least Concern which way the Truth shall be determined. His sole Endeavour has been to discover it; be it what, or where, or how it will: Nor can I hear, without Concern, you, of whose Understanding I would, for the Sake of the Public, wish to think favourably; expressing a Desire that the Government would appoint Persons, *capable* and *indifferent*, such are your Terms, to enquire into the Matter. Who, Sir, are you, that are thus dictating unto the Government? Retire into yourself and know your Station! Who is more *capable*, or who more *indifferent*, than this generous Magistrate? Or has there been among the most violent and misguided of this Creature's Friends, any Man, for I will not suppose you could, but has there been any Man, who has dared to whisper to his own Heart a Thought that it were otherwise?

To this 'tis fit to add, that his Lordship, as *Supreme Magistrate* of that Court in which the Cause was tried, is the proper Person for this Examination: and that he has already finished it. Why should it then be supposed necessary, or why proper, to take the Cognizance of an Affair of this Importance, out of his Hands who has a Right to examine into it: or what would be the Justice, or what the Gratitude, of appointing others to do that which he has done already; and for which he deserves, and for which he will receive, the universal Applause of Mankind!

What is the real Case, with respect to the Girl, Heaven and her own Conscience only; at least I hope they only, know. I have no Right to assert any Thing, nor do: and my Opinion cannot hurt her. There does appear to have been a Conspiracy, and a most foul and black one: It is possible, at least, there may have been such; this her Friends must allow; and she who has certainly accused, and persecuted to the utmost, an innocent Person, whether it hath been ignorantly or designedly, cannot expect she shall escape the Suspicion. That *Squires* is Guiltless is beyond all doubt: That *Canning* was not confined in the House of *Wells* is as much beyond all Possibility of doubting. She appears to have proceeded wilfully: but there is a Possibility she may have done it ignorantly; and the World will be glad for her own Sake, that she could prove it a Mistake; horrible as it will appear even in that Consideration.

Thus stands the whole: And upon this Foundation rests the Innocence of the unhappy Convict. What greater Proof can Innocence require? What greater can it admit! Who is there among ourselves that might not, by the same Artifice, have been accused, and by the same Evidence convicted of the Crime? Or who is there, had he been so accused, that could have brought a fuller Proof of Innocence? I cannot question, but that the Impartial will be convinced: But would all were impartial.

I thought the Public were clear in it before; but what is there so swift as Misinformation? An Indisposition had shut me from the World a few Days, and at the End of that little Period, when I mixed among Men again, what a Change was there in their Opinions! I left them assured, and they had Right to be assured of it, of the Convict's Innocence: I find them full in the Belief that she is Guilty: but I do not wonder at this; nor can I blame the most resolute among them, when I hear the Foundations of the new Opinion. These Delusions, however, are not calculated for Duration: They serve the Purpose till they are exploded; and then who knows the Authors?

Men hear that all which has been told them, concerning the Convict's being in another Place at the Time of the alledged Robbery, has been since discovered to be false. I, who have told them all that related to the Attestation of her being so, do now assure them, that there has been no such Discovery. Nothing has happened to take one Grain from the Weight of any of those Evidences, on which I founded the Opinion; but many, very many Things, to countenance, support, and prove their Truth. Falsities innumerable have been, indeed, devised by the Interested, received by the Credulous, and propagated by the Malicious; but who is there to be found, that will himself attest any the least Circumstance that they pretend?

There are Men, are there not, Mr. *Fielding*? who cannot bear the Glory this will soon bring, and ought to bring, to the great Magistrate who has discovered the Conspiracy. And these will swallow greedily all that they hear against it; and they will propagate that which they don't believe. There are Men, who have been deceived: Who now know they have been deceived; but who are ashamed to own it. A foolish Shame: The seeing the Delusion proved upon them, and it will soon be proved, will be much greater. These will add to the Numbers that are busy in spreading every Breath of Falsehood: and I am sorry to add, there may be some who even on my Account will be as violent to blast the Credit of all that has been doing. Though not conscious that I deserve to have one Enemy in the World, I am not ignorant that I have several; and some of these are of that idle Kind who live in the meaner Coffeehouses, and spread Reports among the successive Companies. These are a Sort of Men, who have not, on any other Occasion, appeared considerable enough to me to justify the slightest Notice; but if their Violence and officious Malice can take any Thing from the Opinion, which the World had entertained of the Credibility of what I have published, designing to be known the Author of it, on this Occasion; I shall for once be sorry that even such Men were my Enemies.

To one or other of these Sets of Persons; all of them mean, wicked, or interested, have been owing the various Reports the World has heard within these few Days upon this Occasion: And not knowing from what Source they have sprung, Men have not known with what Contempt to treat them. The same short Answer serves for all I have heard; and I desire no other than to stand accountable to all who shall dispute that Answer.

I have been told, that the Lord Mayor had given up the Cause, finding all Perjury that had been brought before him: There is no Truth in any Part of this. The Lord Mayor never altered his Opinion; he is convinced by Proof of what he first guessed from Reason: And his Lordship will, as soon as that is proper, convince all the World.

I have been told the Vicar of *Abbotsbury* is, or has been, in Town. There is no Truth in this. That he has contradicted what I have said concerning him: Neither is there in this: On the contrary, he has certified it all in a Letter to a noble Lord, a Letter which you Mr. *Fielding* know of; and that noble Personage also countenances, by his Character of this Gentleman, all that his Conduct in the Matter had before spoken in his Favour.

It has been said that the Certificates and Affidavits in the Lord Mayor's Hands, sent up from *Abbotsbury*, and attested by this Gentleman, and by the Church-wardens and Overseers of the Parish are forged. There is no Truth in this Report, nor the least Shadow of Foundation for it: They are confirmed. 'Tis said the Letters from that Gentleman are forged: They also are authenticated. That the Church-wardens and Overseers mentioned in those Papers are, or have been, in Town, and contradict the whole: This also is wholly untrue; not one of them either has been here, or has contradicted, by Letter, or any other way, any Part of that Evidence: All stands on the full Credit that it did. It has been said, that an Exciseman, now in Town, whose Evidence is in itself sufficient, and is a new Testimony of Truth in all the other's, had undergone a previous Examination by a Gentleman, whom they even dare to name, before he was seen by the Lord Mayor: I have Authority from that Gentleman to declare, that this also is wholly false. And I, on *Monday*, heard the Man himself say, he never saw him, till in the Lord Mayor's Presence. It has been lastly said, that the Recantation of *Virtue Hall* was not taken in a candid and fair Manner by the Lord Mayor himself. Where will Slander stop, when it dares rise to this! All I have seen of that was perfectly fair, and most particularly candid: And it was a happy Precaution the Lord Mayor used, never to speak with her alone.

These are the Stories I have heard; they are related boldly; and they are enough in Number. They are enough to plead in full Excuse for those which have been wavering in their Opinion; and they will be found enough to condemn their Authors, nay, and the busy Propagators of them too, to everlasting Ignominy.

No more can be declared at this Time than I have told; but I shall conclude this, as I have done the other Accounts which I have given of these Proceedings, with assuring those who pay me the Attention of reading it, that the Truth will appear, and that soon; under such Proof, as will do immortal Honour to the Magistrate who has discovered it; will condemn to Shame and Confusion all who have disingenuously opposed it; and will at once, astonish, and convince the World.

For you, Mr. *Fielding*! I have no Right to call your Behaviour as a Magistrate in Question; nor have I Abilities to judge of it: I have, therefore, no where alluded to it: But certainly your private Treatment of this Subject, both before and in your Pamphlet, merits the strongest Censure.

FINIS.